This Is My Body

This Is My Body

Laura Bruce Watt

RESOURCE *Publications* · Eugene, Oregon

THIS IS MY BODY

Copyright © 2022 Laura Bruce Watt. All rights reserved. Except for brief quotations in critical publications or reviews, no part of this book may be reproduced in any manner without prior written permission from the publisher. Write: Permissions, Wipf and Stock Publishers, 199 W. 8th Ave., Suite 3, Eugene, OR 97401.

Resource Publications
An Imprint of Wipf and Stock Publishers
199 W. 8th Ave., Suite 3
Eugene, OR 97401

www.wipfandstock.com

PAPERBACK ISBN: 978-1-6667-5308-0
HARDCOVER ISBN: 978-1-6667-5309-7
EBOOK ISBN: 978-1-6667-5310-3

09/22/22

For my grandparents.
James and Priscilla Mclean, and James and Danella Watt.

"Do you know what a poem is, Esther?"

"No, what?" I would say.

"A piece of dust."

—Sylvia Plath, *The Bell Jar*

"This is My body which is broken for you."

—1 Corinthians 11:24 The Bible NJKV

Contents

Acknowledgements | ix

Body

This Is My Body | 3
Knitted Together | 5
Hereditary | 7
Shoulder | 9
Cocoon | 11
Thank You | 13
Salt | 15
Temple | 17
Impediment | 19
Lemonade | 21
Bones | 24
Ocean | 26
Parma Violets | 28
The Shadow of Death | 30
An Offering | 32

Mind

This Is My Mind | 37
Underwater | 40
L'Appel du Vide | 42
Yellow | 44
Fool | 48
In Your Head | 50
Spiral | 52
Unravel | 54
Field of Flowers | 57

Dirt | 59
Daydreaming | 61
Driving | 62
I Have a Monster | 65
Forget Me Not | 67
Sorry | 71

Soul

This Is My Soul | 75
Daily Bread | 78
Bedtime Prayers | 80
Jonah | 82
Relationship | 84
Battle | 86
We Are More Than Stars | 89
Left Behind | 91
Written in Blood | 93
Sleeping | 95
Mosaics | 97
Tongues | 100
Light | 102
It Is Well | 104
His Body | 106

Acknowledgements

Thank you to Marieann Joy for all your help in bringing this collection to life.

Thank you to my family for always believing in me and for encouraging me in my writing journey.

A special thank you goes out to Monica Jack for all you have done for me. I am so grateful that you have created a safe space for me to come and offload any negative thoughts or feelings that I am experiencing and for working through these with me.

Body

This Is My Body

This is my body,
A claim
In which I have
The truth
In declaring
That I own this.
The shell
That I was
Dragged up in
As I morph.
Growing pains
Mark the heights
That I will
Never reach.
I am but
A girl,
Never fully
Grown up.
This is my body,
I decide,
Or so I thought.
The opinions
Of others
Fog the internal
Monologue.
The voice
In my head
Is clear and free
Of impediment.

I prefer
When I am
Silent.
Most people
Do.
Tripping
Over your own
Name is like
Tripping
Over your own
Two feet,
Which I often do
Too.
This body
Sometimes feels
Heavier
Than it should.
I am carrying
The weight
Of an anxious
Mind
Who feels like
An entity
In itself.

Knitted Together

Knitted hats,
Cardigans, and
Blankets,
All pure
White wool
Woven together by
Fingers so gentle
To ensure
The perfect
Garment.
An expectant
Mother
Sits in a
Wool-draped
Room saying
A silent prayer,
Begging the Lord
To protect
Her little one.
As her eyes
Well,
He breathes
Inward peace.
He sees all
That is to
Come as He
Knits together
Perfectly
The inmost parts

Of the
Little one
Held within
A faithful mother.
Like the
Hands that
Knit woolen gifts,
How wonderfully
He crafts
His creation,
Passing down
Mother's eyes
And father's patient
Nature,
All sealed with
God's promise
To protect
And be present.
How blessed
Are we
To know
That this is
How we
Are formed,
In His perfect way.
Children
Are a gift from
The Lord,
Fruit of the womb,
A reward
Of your faithfulness,
All created in
His image.

Hereditary

I hold
A sparkle
Of mischief
Within my eyes.
Brown eyes
Have a subtle
Beauty,
Deep enough
To get lost in.
My eyes
Are not
Only my own.
Passed down by
My grandfather
From those who
Came before,
My iris is
A time capsule,
Locking in generations.
One day
I too hope
To pass down
That glisten
Of wonder.
To be responsible
For the birthright.
The eyes that
I searched for
At the school gate,

Sparkling as they
Found mines.
On the night
You had another
Heart-attack,
I could not
Meet them.
I was scared
But you were not.
They are
The bravest eyes
I have ever
Stared into.
I did not know
The power
They held
Until
I saw the fire
In my own eyes
On nights
I nearly fell
Apart.
I remember on
Late drives
You would sing to
The moon.
You told me
It could see
Me too,
But the only eyes
I cared about
Were ours.

Shoulder

I was fourteen
When I was told
To cover up
My shoulders
In church.
As if
The meat
On my bones
Was enough
To render
Sinful temptation.
It is not a man's
Fault nor blame.
Lust
Is a hunger
That grows
Inside him.
That is what
They told me.
The mouths
Of saints
Water
By virtue of
The temptress's
Subtle seduction.
From the meat
On her bones,
You could
Feed a

Crowd of
Five thousand men.
They feast on
The flesh
She dares
To bare.
It is her
Fault.
They were
Starving and
She offered
Her body
As a
Sacrifice.

Cocoon

Under the bedsheets,
In a cocoon of
Comfort,
I cry.
Here I hide
From the constant
Inescapable fear.
Metamorphosis
Fails me as I
Emerge unchanged.
I am alone
Under the covers,
Like when
I was young
And I hid
From the monsters.
The monsters
Under the bed.
The monsters
Awake in my head.
Dark clouds
And thunderstorms
All arrive
In my room.
Like the
Day of the dead,
My demons
Come out of
Their graves

In a hurricane of
Self-loathing
And regret.
I am tormented
By my thoughts
Yet I pretend
That I am okay.
I laugh
And my voice
Cracks at the end.
Self-destructive behavior,
Ever indulged
Until the next purge
Is set.
Caterpillar bile
Seeps from
Underneath.
The tears
Will not cease
As they mix
With the poison.
Cracks and disjoints
Revealing
A broken-winged
Butterfly,
Torn at the edges,
Damned
To suffocate
Beneath blankets.

Thank You

They take my
Blood
And I say
Thank you.
Rolled up sleeves,
Veins concealed in
Porcelain,
Blue,
Too hard to
See.
Roses in liquid
Form
Spill into
Needles embedded
In skin as
Plasters are speckled
With petals,
Add pressure
To stop the flow
As pressure is
Added
To my chest.
Red fills tubes,
Dated and printed.
Needles in arms
Every second month,
Appointment cards
Guide me home
To the blood bank

Running me
Dry.
I lost
My blood
Over the years
So a stranger
Gave me theirs.
I am grateful
For their loss
Which in turn
Is my gain.
They take my
Blood
And I say
Thank you.

Salt

The doubt of
Lot's wife
Turned her
Into a pillar of
Salt.
I too
know
What it is
To disintegrate.
Daily,
Doubt captures me,
In the grit.
Stinging
My skin,
Rough to touch.
Saltwater seeps
From pores
As I become
A pillar
Of my own
Disbelief.
I am the salt
That pours from
My eyes,
Dissolving the rest
Of me.
You intended us
To be
Salt of

The earth
Yet
Here I am
Just
Salt
Sinking
Into the ground
Loosing flavor
And losing purpose.

Temple

I am crumbling,
Rock and rubble
All around.
There is no
Beauty to
Display
Here.
A temple
Devoid of
Treasure,
Just an
Ancient ruin
Struggling to stay
Upright.
The body
Is a temple,
A holy place.
Yet mine
Is a wreckage.
A thief came
And robbed me
Of the riches
Within,
Over time
Taking
Piece by piece
Until I am
Nothing
But stone.

Deteriorating
From
The foundations,
I am one
More crack
Away from
Burial,
Like Samson
Regaining
His strength.
Soon
I will be
Embalmed
In the
Brokenness
Of my own
Body.

Impediment

When I open
My mouth
There is a disconnect
Between
The sweet melody
Of eloquent
Sentences
I want
To deliver
And the words
That clamber out
Instead.
My voice lets me
Down.
My cupid's bow
Carves beautiful
Disaster,
Daring not to get
Too close
As my tongue
Trips over
Itself.
It renders me
Silent
When I have
So much
To say.
I cannot bear
The thought

Of my
Own voice.
I wonder if it
Was inflicted
Upon me
To keep me
Out of trouble,
Like a thorn
Found firmly planted
In my mouth.
I run my tongue
Across it,
Forgetting
Each time
How much it hurts.
My mouth
Filling
With the taste
Of iron,
Like an anchor
Weighing me down.
I splutter
Out words,
Choking on
My own
Inarticulation.

Lemonade

I am not
Who I was
Back then,
But there is a
Part of her
Layered beneath
Who I am
Now.
A labyrinth
Of my past
Self
Hidden in the
Core of me.
She is a stranger
To the skin
She dwells in.
The new skin
Suffocates
As it binds in the
Hurt.
If you met
Me at eighteen,
You may not
Know me,
But you do,
All the same.
Smiles crack
Like mirrors
That fall,

Seven years
Of bad luck,
Seven years
Of the girl
I once was.
She claws from
Within,
Pulling apart
As I rebuild.
Washed out
And washed down
With something
Bitter.
Life gave you lemons,
You made lemonade.
I spiral downwards,
That bittersweet
Disinfectant
Failing to purge.
Drinking lemon
Bleach
Still
Would not
Clear the inside
Of the girl
I used to be.
I am infected
By myself.
Years
Of destruction
Fester beneath
The surface
Until they reach
This point
Where I cannot
Bear

My own conscience.
Rose-tainted nostalgia,
Scrubbed
With bleach,
Now a weaker
Pastel.
Dull out
The inner voice
That mocks,
"It will get better."
It never does.
The ocean
Guides
My every move
As I find myself
Waist deep
And walking
Forward,
Disappearing into saltwater.
My wounds sting,
All reopened
From the past.
Salt-water pours
But
Like bleach,
Nothing
Can cleanse
That deep.

Bones

My skeleton
Clambers
Out of the closet
Like it has
A secret to tell.
I am afraid
That I may
Let you down.
I am not enough.
Porcelain,
I will break
If held too long.
My bones
All drowning
In the same skin,
Limb after limb
But nothing
Is ever
Beyond skin deep.
You cannot see
My soul.
I am just a body
To you.
Tap and make a
Wish
Upon hollow
Collarbones.
I throw my bones
To you.

Will that be enough?
You love me,
You love me
Not.
Throwing bones
Like petals,
I pick apart.
Fragments
Puncture my insides
As the
Internal sabotage
Begins.
Acid spills from
Organs,
Rage in liquid
Form.
I am drowning
From the inside
Out.
I am captive to
My own ribcage,
Outnumbered
As I continue
To throw
My bones to you.
I pile on the floor
Yet I am still
Overwhelmed.
My spine breaks
Through the skin,
Exposing
That which
I lack
As I pick apart.

Ocean

I cannot get out
Of the ocean
If I am the
Ocean.
I drown in all
Of me.
As the internal
Waves crash,
I forget
That I am
Perishable.
I am fragile
In my shell.
Some days
I am
Only a body,
As I sink
To places
My mind
Would never go.
On those
Days
I am reminded
Of how mortal
I am.
Of how mortal
We all are.
If the mountains
Are in heaven,

Let me
Stay in the seas.
I am not ready
To go.

Parma Violets

Parma Violets
Lay open
On the bedside
Cabinet.
A symbol
Of childhood
Innocence,
Now a looming
Reminder
Of the pills
You never take
But just
A little sweeter.
Pastel pale, as
Violet delights
Have violent ends.
Pass a packet
While they
Shot back
The Sunday wine.
You are too young
To understand.
Eat your sweets,
It will be fine.
They are
More saccharine
Than the sour
They devour,
Confessing sins

From days past.
Dissolving tablets,
On tongues
Whilst they
Take of the body.
Cannibals
Swallowing
Shallow portions
With much more
Shallow intentions
Until it is time
Once more
To take
The table
Before our Lord.

The Shadow of Death

The shadow of
Death
Is the darkest
Place.
A black bird
Extends
Her wings
Over us all,
Cradling us here
Where you are
Paralyzed,
Choking on feathers,
Struggling
For breath.
I waste a lungful
Just sitting here,
Talking at you.
If your eyes
Flicker,
I make believe
That they say
"I love you."
Death has her
Claws
Dug deep
Into your chest,
Stuttering the rhythm.
Her rattle
Rises in your throat,
A reminder

That time
Is running out.
I imagine
He is already
Here to
Remind Death
That she
Does not
Hold power
For long.
His rod and staff
Parked by
Your bedpost,
Waiting to walk
The last steps
Through
The valley
With you.
As dark as
It may seem,
It is simply
A shadow
Where life meets
Its end.
But there
Is more
On the other side.
Your body
Could not
Continue here.
Morphine only
Numbs pain
For so long.
But in His
Glory you
Will be restored.

An Offering

Palms open,
Empty,
There is nothing
I can give
But this shell.
My body offered
To you.
For what
Purpose
Is there but
To be yours?
On the altar,
I lie.
It is not
Much
But it
Is all I have.
These hands
Will write
Of your love.
I am unworthy
Of your mercy
Yet it is given
Daily.
My breath
Belongs
Only to you.
For years I wasted
Air,

Blowing smoke
Into the unknown
When all I had
To do was praise.
As fear chases,
Seeking
To throw me
Off course,
I will go where
You direct
My path.
Footprint by
Footprint,
I tread lightly
Through doorways
Only you can
Open.
This is my body,
But I give it to
You.

Mind

This Is My Mind

I am a prisoner
Within my
Mind.
Caught up
In the actions
Of years ago.
Captive to
How I felt that
Night
And how it
Was my fault.
Everything
Is my fault.
I layer salt
Into wounds
Of days
Gone by
In an act
Of preservation.
The wound
Never fails to
Sting.
The hurt
Reminds me
That it happened,
Like a scrapbook
Of salvaged
Forget-me-nots.
The videotape

Never
Wears out
In my mind.
The movie
Replays
As I scream,
Feeling the pain
All over
Again.
I cannot
Drown out
Her negativity,
Only His word
Can.
He can calm the
Tempest
Within,
While I wipe
The tears
Of saltwater
Streaming from
My face.
He comes in a
Prayer,
Bleaching
The memories
Of the mistakes
I made,
Which He
Forgot years ago.
He cast that
Burden away
Back when
I asked Him
To.
Why then do

I choose
To carry it around,
Reveling
In trauma
When He can
Wipe it all
Clean?
This is my mind,
But I wish
It was His.

Underwater

I know
I am slipping
Under again.
The waves are
Pulling,
Dragging my body
Across grit and sand.
Salt stings my
Eyes
As I sink
A little lower
Than before.
I try to breathe,
Choking
On water.
Spiraling downwards,
I am anchored
By the tide.
The waves
Call me home.
A shell
Held to my ear
Whispers
To let go,
Let the ocean
Take you,
Let go and
Breathe in
The effluent.

Salt burns
The back of
My throat
As I scream.
My eyes scratch
At the surface
As sand pulls
Across me.
Clothes
Filled with water,
Pulling me down
And down
And farther still
Until I am nearly
One
with the
Ocean floor,
The bed
I call my home.
An uneasy
Ruin
Of broken shell
And shattered glass.
Damned beauty
Of the
Broken dreams
And potential
I will never realize.

L'Appel du Vide

The call of the void.
A bleak echo
Stirs the internal
Hurricane.
Why would I do that?
Thoughts creep in
Like an itch begging
To draw blood,
Never satisfied until
I submit.
As I peel back the skin
Around my nails.
Peeling
Every thought of you,
Cleansing
My flesh from
Your touch
Until blood pours
And my inside
Is exposed.
Insight warns
Of danger ahead
Like headlights
On night roads.
My heart pounds
As I stomp.
Foot to the
Pedal,
Down to the floor.

Six feet
Down to the floor.
I walk
At the cliff edge
And I am blind
To the scenery.
But I feel
The earth
Shifting,
Calling my feet
Forward
Until I am throwing
My body
Down
To the
Ocean waves.
Breath heavy and
Lungs full
Under the bath water.
The call of the void.
L'Appel du vide.
I am self-destruction.
Cigarettes blacken
My lungs and
Alcohol burns at
My throat.
Blackout, blackout, blackout,
Until I am the void.

Yellow

I cried a river
And
It sunk me.
I was drowning
Under my
Tears.
The river ran
Blue.
A shower of
Sadness
I could
Not shift.
All I can
Do is
Put on
Yellow,
And try
To
Color correct
The sad tones
Staining my mood,
To block
Out blue
With
A golden hue.
I am
Rather childish
In my beliefs
That a color

Can save me.
Like a childhood
Memory.
Holding buttercups
To chins
To say I like you
Too.
That theory
Has yet
To let me down,
Unless you
Count the time
My hair
Was neon.
Everyone
Hated it,
But I felt so
Happy.
I felt yellow.
Like Van Gogh
I would consume
Poison,
Yellow paint,
Burned his
Throat
Because he knew
What it was
To want to
Be yellow
From the inside out.
And I know he
Never really did
That.
But I still know
What it feels like
To want

To.
Even if the world
Thinks
You are insane.
I settle for
Nail varnish
And clothing
Of a similar
Lemon tinge.
I cannot bear
Anything
But
Yellow.
I try to
Convince
Myself
These
Primary colors
Will not merge
Into a
Muddy
Khaki mess.
At least
If they do
I can cover
Myself
In the camouflage
That I create.
Everything I hate
Is blue.
Bruises on arms
Linger,
Yellow
After purple
Fades
From blue.

There is no
Yellow when
The lights
Dim.
What faith
To store
In that of
A watercolor
Possibility.
That yellow will
Make
Everything
Blue
Disappear.

Fool

She is to
Be a fool.
A beautiful
Damned fool,
For that is all
A girl is good for.
Yet a fool
I will never be again.
I have been
A goodnight
Kiss,
Politely brushing
Lips to pass the
Day to night.
I have been
Numbing
Nights,
Throwing myself
Upon the fire
To keep warm.
I have been
Hurricanes
Of the words
You unleashed upon me.
I have been the
Girl
I never intended
To be.
I have been

The shooting
Star,
Falling at
The windowpane.
I have been the
Forgotten
Eyes on the
Dancefloor.
A forgotten touch
As the daylight creeps in.
I am nobody's
Baby.
I belong to
No one.
I belong to
Nothing
But my own twisted
Memory,
Smile back
At the mischief
And wipe
A tear
For the
Phantom
Touch,
Rendered upon
A beautiful
Little
Fool.

In Your Head

It is all
In your head.
What is not
Real
Cannot
Hurt you.
But what if
The twister
Swirling
Around my head
Is real?
The fog
Clogs
Up my brain.
I cannot see
Through the darkness.
I am one
With the abyss.
Everything blurs
Together
Into the shape
Of my greatest
Fears.
It is in
My mind,
But that does not
Mean that it
Is not real.
I am scared,

Stuck
In this place,
Caught up
In the storm's destruction.
I cannot separate it
From myself.
The thoughts
Latch
Onto
Who I am,
Redefine how
I see the mirror
Image.
I will never be more
Than my thoughts.
I am overwhelmed,
Yet ferociously
Numb
To the things
I hear
In my head.

Spiral

Spiraling,
I am pulled
Inwards.
I separate
At the seams.
My cords
Loosen.
Heart strings
Snap
As I break
Apart
Until there is only
A thread left.
One thread
Holding together
This illusion
That I am
Fine.
But even
That
Wears thin
In the middle
Of the
Spiral.
It is getting bad again.
I am bad again.
I smile,
Cracking a few
Bones in the

Process.
As I laugh,
Begging my body
To be
Okay.
I feel my blood
Slow,
Trickling through veins.
On the surface
I am blue.
Anemic.
Breathing
Does not come
Easy
Anymore.
I whisper
To the tears,
My voice a
Lullaby,
Soothing as they fall.
As I fall
Deeper
Into the labyrinth
Of myself,
Where the past
Curdles the present.
Sweet
Consumed by the
Bitter.
The spiral always
Recoils before
It throws me out,
And I am left
Dizzy
On the comedown.

Unravel

The bundle of
Wool
In my brain
Is all
Tangled up,
Stubborn in
Its labyrinth.
It has become
Too heavy
To carry
Around.
I need
Someone to help
Unpack
The mess.
I sit
Cross-legged
On a sofa
Across from
Someone who
Promises she will
Not judge,
And in my
Cynical nature
I try
To believe her.
We work section
By section.
Her questions are

Open enough
For me to
Lead the way,
Yet direct
Enough
That I cannot
Hide
The things
That matter most.
Somewhere, knitted
Up in a corner,
Are all the things
I have been
Too scared
To say out loud.
To find the
Source of this
Muddle
We unpick
Enough knots
Around it.
There is purpose
As we unravel
The bundle,
As her fingers
Untangle
The thoughts
I cannot understand
On my own.
We end
With a prayer
As time has
Gone again.
But as I leave
My mind feels
Clear.

I understand it
Better than
I did
Before.
I may re-tangle
Over time
But when I do
We can
Work together
To pick
At the knots.

Field of Flowers

In a field
Of flowers,
I stood
Staring at
Fallen petals.
Their colors
Faded as
They lay
There dying.
Daisy chains
Held me down,
A fallen princess
Without
Her crown.
So close to beauty,
Still fallen too far.
A broken mind,
Peace she
Cannot find.
In a haze
Of yellow days,
Beauty leaves,
Decayed like those
From trees.
Beauty of spirit
But
Not of mind.
Ugliness stems
Deep inside.

Thorns do grow
In gardens slow.
The princess's
Tears flow,
Feeding the garden
To help it grow.
It is never
As dark as
It may seem.
You are not
Broken,
Nor are you
Chained.
Uproot the fear,
Uproot the doubt.
Your kingdom
Is always
Yours to reign.
Even in
Sadness.
Even in
Pain.

Dirt

I feel the earth
Beneath
My fingernails.
In the flowerbed,
I am growing
And destroying
All at once.
Among the seeds
I have planted,
I impatiently
Pull apart
Everything I have built.
Even nostalgia
Is no longer
Tinted rose.
I am unable to
Grow anything of
Beauty.
I await
The flowers' bloom
To witness
Something
That I have created,
Something good
To stem from
The darkness
In which I dwell.
No sunlight to nourish,
No sunlight to feed.

I suffocate
My dreams
And stomp on
The garden
Until there
Is nothing
But weeds
Weaving
Their way around
My ankles,
Pulling me down
To the thorns
To lay.

Daydreaming

If I dream
At all,
Let it be
In the day,
As I walk
Forward
Into realities
My dreams cannot
Even fathom.
In steps
Of the sleepwalker,
I pace on,
Yawning
As I go.
The daydream
So good,
I cannot
Fall asleep
At night.
I am living
My wildest dreams
Come true.
Yet I dream
Of more.
My mind will
Not settle
Where I am,
For I know that
The best
Is yet to come.

Driving

Somewhere
Deep inside
Is the wriggling
Feeling
That this is going
Too well.
The self-destructive
Demon
Begs to be
Right,
Waiting
To say
"I told you so,"
To the angel
Sat upon
My shoulder,
Wiping away
The tears
That shower
Upon her.
The storm
Is so loud
It drowns
Out her soft
Whisper of,
"It will all be okay."
Instead an anthem
Of self-loathing
Plays

On repeat,
Fueled by the demon's
Taunts.
It sneers,
Rejoicing in the
Pain that takes
Over,
Until I am numb.
Crack a smile
To the crowds,
And with that
I crack a thousand
Bones in the
Process.
The world pointing
At the reasons
Why I am selfish.
Can I not see
How lucky
I am?
But in
That moment
All I see are headlights
Glaring.
I envision
My car at
The roadside.
I see the unforgivable.
I see the grief.
And I know
That I cannot.
But in that moment,
I am
Numb enough
That
I do not care.

When
The demons are driving,
Destruction
Is the only
Destination.

I Have a Monster

I have a monster
Who lives within,
Creeping out,
At the worst of times.
I take credit
For her
Bad habits
As they mark me
With all the
Chaos
She brings.
My potential is
Her fuel
To do no good.
She is lazy
And slothful as
She creeps in
At unknown hours,
Rousing my mind,
Voiding
The daylight hours.
As I wake
In the afternoon,
They will laugh
And say
"That is just like you."
I wipe a tear
Hoping tomorrow
I will do better.

She listens
To songs
That keep her low,
Taking me
With her as
She sneers
That I will never
Be more
Than her bad days.
She laughs along
With the disappointed
Yet unsurprised
Crowd,
Who are
"Used to me by now,"
And takes
No credit
For the sins
She bestows up me.
Please believe me
When I say,
I have a monster.

Forget Me Not

I hope she
Never forgets me,
But if she
Does,
I hope she
Knows
That I will
Not forget her.
Sipping cups
Of tea,
Only ever drank
From a
China cup,
She would
Smile as
It would
Clink
Against
Her teeth.
Laughing, she
Would tell me
How she
Still has
All her own
And I would
Act surprised,
Like she was
Telling me for
The first time.

I would listen
To her stories
Over and over
Again
To hear
The excitement
In her voice.
She lives
In a month
Full of Sundays,
Asking everyday
If we have
Been out
To the meeting.
I know
That, even if
She forgets
Us all,
She will never
Forget
Her Lord.
Scripture stored
Deep in her
Memory,
Even as the
Rest grows
Hazy.
She
Can recite
The verses
Word for word.
She may
Be growing
Older,
But I see
Her growing

Down
As her brain
Wanes
Childlike.
As she Looks
For her father,
I see the
Fear
Creep across
My grandfather's
Face.
He knows
We do not
Have long left
In her mind.
I would like
To stay
A while
Longer,
If she does
Not mind.
Forget me not,
I pray
As
I wipe my
Tears with
A handkerchief
Passed down
From
Her collection.
I do not
Think I have
Ever seen her
Cry,
For she is braver
Than I could

Ever be.
Her mind
Becomes
A stranger,
Yet she laughs
In the face
Of this unknown
Danger.

Sorry

I am sorry
For thinking
This way.
Disobedient
To the thought
Processes
You would carve
Out for me.
I am a work
In progress,
Unfinished
On this earth.
But one day
I will think in
The way
That you
Intended.
After the Fall,
There was room
For thoughts
To creep in.
Thoughts of evil,
That you never
Destined
Your people
To hold
In their minds.
Whispered
From the enemy,
Convincing them

To eat.
The option to
Say no
Was always there.
The option
To drive out
The thoughts
Feels void
But it is there.
Let your mind
Be renewed
Daily
In the promises,
Even
If you do not
Believe them
In the moment.
Keep declaring
Over the darkness
And soon
It will flee.
There will be a
Day
When my mind
Will be free.
But
On this earth
There may
Be darker days
To come.
I am sorry
For those
Days
When I doubt
Who you
Made me
To be.

Soul

This Is My Soul

This is my soul,
Suffocated deep
Within my body,
Forced to decipher
The thoughts
Of my mind
Into emotions.
When the body
Withers
And the mind
Forgets in old age
The soul remains
Consistent.
It is steadfast,
But it serves
Me no purpose
To keep
Hold of it.
I surrendered it
To Him.
For what
Shall a man
Profit
If he gains
The whole
World
But loses
His soul?
I have seen

Bodies buried
And I know
They cannot
Take a thing
To the grave,
Not even
Secrets
As there
Are no
Secrets
From the
Omniscient Father.
He knows
My soul's
Desire
To do better.
When my mind
Let's me down
It is hard
For my body
Not to
Follow
And give into
The actions
Of a sinner.
In doing so
I forget
Who you
Created
Me to be.
I will
Do better
Next time,
I promise
In a prayer.
My name

Is written
In the
Book of Life
And no one
Shall remove it.
My soul is yours
Forevermore
And for that
I am thankful.
I continue
To drown
In self-doubt
Yet you only
Wish to
Baptize me
In your grace,
Restoring my
Soul
Each time.
This is my soul,
Yet I gladly
Give it for Him
To be its keeper.

Daily Bread

Give us today
Our daily bread.
A prayer request
For substance,
Not only
Of stomach
But of soul.
The Lord preached
That the body
Cannot survive
On bread
Alone
But that
The soul
Should be fed
By the word
Of God.
Yet I am pulling
Green mold
From the corners
Of scraps.
Surviving on
The Bible verses
Chimed
In childhood
And sustaining
Faith on
Bygone
Miracles

Can only feed
The soul
For so long.
The soul
Is malnourished
Begging
For wisdom
And new understanding
Of the word.
Open it daily
To soak in
His truth.

Bedtime Prayers

Bedtime prayers,
Quoted word for word.
I cannot go
To sleep without
You,
Like the teddy bear
Held tight
To my chest.
These words I feared
Most
Because of the weight
Of my bedtime
Chant.
"As I lay down,
My head to sleep.
I pray the LORD,
My soul to keep.
For if I die before
I wake,
I Pray the LORD
My soul
To take."
After reciting
I would lie
Awake,
Terrified of the
Deal I had
Made.
Too young to
Comprehend

The cost of forever.
Staying awake
As long as possible,
Terrified that
The Lord would
Accept my offer
And take
My soul
In the night.
I did not wish
To die then,
Although
When I did
In later years
In life,
I knew He
Would not
Keep the
Promise,
Not if
I handed Him
My soul.
Yet still
I whispered
The words,
Taking sleeping pills,
Using
The prayer
As my chaser.
Begging the Lord
To save me
From myself.
Asking Him
To take my soul.
Hoping I would not
Wake.

Jonah

Throw me
Out to sea.
I am going
The wrong way.
God knows it
And has cast
A storm.
There is method
In the madness.
This destruction
Chases me
Away from
Greater hurt.
Jonah
Made his way
Into the depths
Believing he
Would meet
His end
But found refuge.
The belly
Of a fish
Is the darkest
Place to survive
But it is safer
Than
The ocean floor.
In hindsight,
I can see

All I was
Saved from.
In the belly of
The darkest nights
I cried out,
Raising
The SOS call.
It was then
I was swallowed
Into His presence.
The peace
Of my rescuer
Was all around.
He was there
Even when I had
Taken the wrong
Turn.
He was there
To help me
Deal with
The fallout
Of my choices
As I made
My way back
To the shore.

Relationship

Religion
Broke my heart.
I was never
Good enough.
A sinner,
Scrubbing my hands
Clean
Only to pick
Up more regrets.
I fall short,
Falling to purge.
Relapsing
Into sin.
Like a dog
I return to
Vomit
While refusing
To acknowledge
My folly.
I could not
Do good
For doing bad.
It consumed me.
Every self-doubting
Thought is
Another sin to add
To the list.
I kept score
Of all the reasons

I was inadequate
When
All He wanted
Was to put His
Arms around me
And cleanse me
Himself.
I am a body
For now
But in that
I have a soul
Which has accepted
Him
And with that
I can call out,
Knowing
That I am never
Too bad
To be saved.

Battle

There is a battle
On-going
For my soul.
This fight is more
Than flesh
And blood,
It is deeper
In its destruction.
For it is a matter
Of life
And death.
There is no
Power in the
Dark
But it disorientates
Even the strongest
Into feeling
Too weak
To vanish it.
The devil
Comes for tea,
Like a storybook
Villain
He charms
His way in.
At first
He tempts with
An apple
Feeding doubt

By the teaspoon.
Before you notice
He is feeding
You a full meal,
Dining
At your table.
His sugar-coated lies
Rot your teeth
As you consume
His deceit.
He freezes you
From the inside,
Slowly enough
That you almost
Do not notice
As he melts you
Into mere
Lukewarm water
To be gargled in
The mouth
Of your Lord.
He then finds
Someone
To provoke you
Or something
To break your
Back,
As he has you
Contorted
Into the
Most awkward
Version
Of yourself,
Spiteful and easily
Offended.
He knows exactly

How to lure
As he slithers in,
Planting seeds
Of doubt.
Do not let him
Reap the benefits
Of his destruction,
Drown him
Out with
The blood
Of the Lamb.
Your savior
Continues
To save you.
Even after salvation,
The battle continues
For your soul.

We Are More Than Stars

I have a birth mark
On my neck.
Like a constellation of stars
It can be joined
Dot to dot.
God is a star-breather.
When He spoke
The universe
Into creation,
He breathed
And it
Was there.
Adam was formed
From the dust
Of the ground.
He was there in
Form
But he had no
Life until
God breathed
It into him.
The stars on
My neck
Are God-breathed
Just as much
As the stars
In the sky,
But they
Are more beautiful.

When you see a
Shooting star
Fall
It is exploding.
As charming
As it may look,
It is their damning.
A suicidal star
Cast from
The heavens above.
There must be
So much pressure
In being
The breath of God.
I know I have
Felt that.
At least I have
Assurance
That we are more
Than stars.

Left Behind

My first anxious
Memories
Are of running
Out of school
Seeking the security
Of my car.
Because if I
Saw my parents,
Then I must be safe.
If the Lord was to
Come back,
He would not
Leave them behind.
But
The state
Of my own soul
Was questionable.
Back then
I gave my heart
Week after week
And prayed
For forgiveness
After every
Unfavorable word.
I did not
Understand
God's grace
But I had grasped fear,
Or rather it

Had grasped
Me.
I was so afraid
Of being left
On an
Earth,
Void of my
Savior.
Insecure
In my salvation,
Not believing
That the price
Had been paid.
When He said
"It is finished!"
He meant it,
Even if I lied
About going to
The sweet shop
After school.
He paid for that
Sin too.
What joy
There is
In the soul's
Security
And the maturity
To understand
I am safe in
His hand.

Written in Blood

At eighteen
My body
Did not
Have enough
Blood.
I was drying out
From the inside,
My heart lugging
Around the little
Life it had left
To keep me going,
With just enough
Hope to get
Me through
The night.
Church congregations
Filled my lungs,
I breathed
In borrowed air
And forgot
My maker
Until it was
Sunday again.
Anemic
In blood and
Faith alike.
I was rushed
To hospital
Where the blood

Of two strangers
Was transfused
Into mine,
Enough to make
Me whole again.
I think my maker
Topped me up
With His blood
That day too.
For I arose
In a new city,
In a new season.
I prayed
That I would be
Made whole.
I think that
Prayer was
Answered
But not how
I envisioned it.
Blood tests
Every second month,
Still fill my calendar
But it is a reminder
That He is not
Finished with me
Yet.

Sleeping

"Make room,
For the girl
Is not dead
But sleeping,"
He declares,
When everyone
Else sees only
Death.
Her eyes closed,
Breathing slowed,
To her,
His voice is
Only a whisper.
The crowd's judgement
Too loud for her
To bear.
She is dead,
Lifeless,
The grave may
As well become
Her home.
Yet He can see
She still holds
Life inside her.
He banishes the
Mockers, silences
Their cries,
Breathes life upon
Her deathbed

And allows her
To rise.
Arise sleepy
Dreamer,
Come out of your slumber.

Mosaics

Broken pieces,
Scattered
On temple floors.
A wreckage
In front of
My maker.
He sees the pieces
Laid before him,
Recognizes them all.
He knew when he
Formed me
How beautiful
My life would be.
Even though nostalgia
Feels like a
Ruby-red tint
Rather than
A pastel-pink.
Looking back
At a blood bath,
I can tell you
The story
Behind each cut.
Every word
That was ever said.
Hypocritical forgiveness,
I can take it
But do you know what
They did to me?
My maker nods and sighs,

He made them too.
He is sorry for
Their sin.
Sent His son to
Take it upon Himself.
Who am I to hold a grudge,
When heaven holds
No blame on me.
My maker did not intend
For man to chip
Away at His
Masterpiece.
He wanted
To bestow
Beauty upon
All His creation.
I once was a stained glass,
Depicting the perfect
Scene.
Over the years,
The pressure can
Build.
Glass can only
Take so much.
I do not
Know
What caused the
Last shatter.
But I know I felt it.
Picking up the pieces,
Glass splitters
Pressing into
Bloody palms,
Held up
Towards
My maker.

He took them all,
Wiped the blood
And cleansed
My wounds.
While the angels
Dried my pieces,
Free of scarlet pools.
My maker took them
All and began to rearrange.
While I shed a tear,
He was pleased
When He was done.
He created something
Perfect out of all the
In between.
Making art out of pain
Is what He does
For me.
When I saw
The finished piece,
It still looked
Fragmented
But He whispered
It will all make
Sense,
You will see.
My maker
Is an artist
And I the art.
Even in my
Mosaic form,
There is beauty
To withhold
In the broken pieces.
Purpose
Built together
Again.

Tongues

Told to speak
Only in tongues
Of angels,
Yet I can barely
Speak without
Tripping over
My own.
Fumbling words,
As they get stuck.
When I open
My mouth,
You remind me
What lips are for.
Lip service,
Letting prayers
Roll off the tongue
In eloquent murmurs
Yet I cannot even
Speak your name,
Lord.
I am tongued tied
And awkward,
Wishing to thank
My maker
But I cannot say
The words.
The same tongue
I wish to praise
You with,

Used to slander
The body
You gave me,
Used to speak
Death to
This mind.
Sometimes I think
You gave me this
Impediment
So that I would
Hold my tongue.
Let my soul
Speak directly.
Do not let
The doubts
Of my mind
Interrupt
What my soul is
Trying
To articulate.

Light

You light a candle
At my feet,
Enough to see
Less than a footstep.
I must follow in
Your prints.
You have seen
My struggle
And you know
The sound
Of my heart-cry.
Tears roll
Like the
Waves you part
Before me.
I can rest on you
And you
Uphold me
When I cannot
Go on.
I am a failure
Yet
You see a future.
I cannot see
Vast and wide
And I do not
Want to,
For if I knew
What all was

To come
In advance,
It would have
Destroyed me.
Your light said
Come
And I followed,
I found myself
Home.
Exactly where
I needed to be
In this season.
You knew what
I needed and
You know why
I struggle at times
To feel anything
And sometimes I feel
Everything
Within
My very bones.

It Is Well

You speak
Right to my
Soul,
The part of
Me that exists
Deep within
The shell
Projected
To the world.
I invited
You in to
Fill up the
Reservoir of
My soul.
Now I have
A well
Deep within
Where living water
Flows
And my portion
Runs over.
Overflowing,
Water rushes through
My rib cage
In its broken
Attempts
Of acting
As a dam,
Waterlogging

The rest
Of me.
Baptized in your
Presence
I am washed
Clean.

His Body

This is my body,
Broken
In front of you.
This is my body,
Drawn out
Before
You all.
Saying grace
To bless all
Including he
Who will
Go on
To deceive me.
This is my
Body.
Feast
Upon the skin.
Drink in the
Liquid,
Ruby red,
Poured out
For you.
My body is
A sacrifice
Given
So that I could
Save your soul.
Nails pierced
Into hands and feet

For you
To go free.
Skin ripped
Open
As they flogged
And mocked.
A crown of thorns
Upon my head,
Yet I am no
Less of a king.
My body
Knew pain
While my mind
Felt endless
Torment.
One of my closest
Sold me for silver,
Yet through it
All I can save
Your soul.
A sacrifice
Of sinless
Self for a
Sin-filled
World.
I became
A body so that
You could find comfort
Within your
Soul.